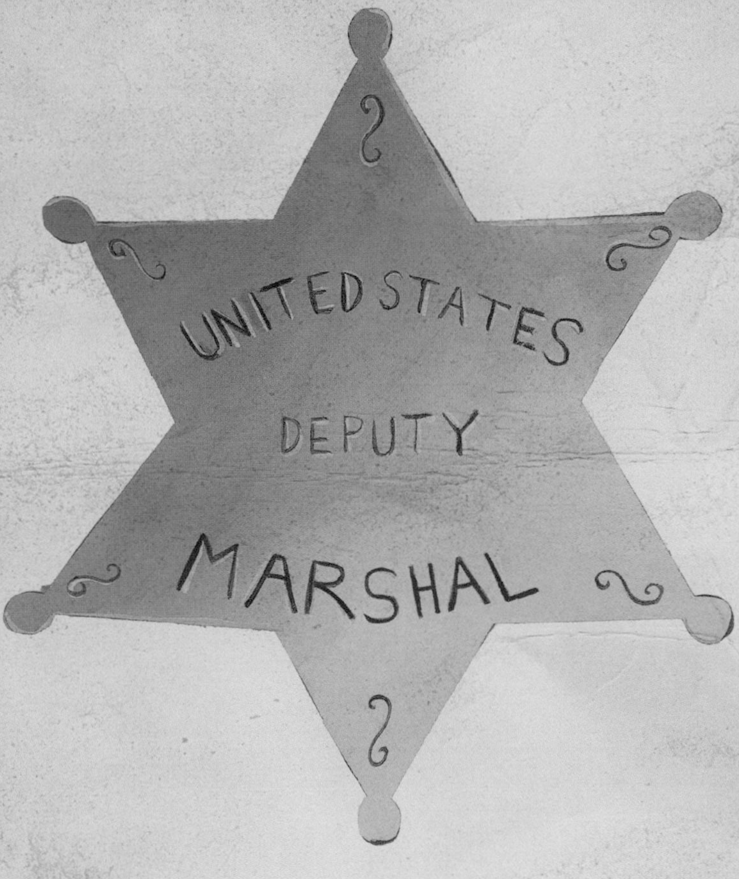
UNITED STATES
DEPUTY
MARSHAL

BAD NEWS
for
OUTLAWS

The REMARKABLE LIFE *of* BASS REEVES, DEPUTY U.S. MARSHAL

Vaunda Micheaux Nelson

ILLUSTRATIONS BY
R. Gregory Christie

Carolrhoda Books M

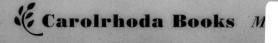

I'm much obliged to historian Art T. Burton for sharing his knowledge and for his fierce commitment to giving Bass Reeves the recognition he so deserves. To my editors, Shannon Barefield and Mary Rodgers; my agent, Tracey Adams; and to pards Kris Sporcic, Stephanie Farrow, Lucy Hampson, Katherine Hauth, Uma Krishnaswami, Jeanne W. Peterson, Lori Snyder, Marilyn Schroeder, and Stephanie Zaslav, I say thank you kindly. Most of all, I'm beholden to my husband, Drew, with whom I'll go to the end of the trail. —V.M.N.

Text copyright © 2009 by Vaunda Micheaux Nelson
Illustrations copyright © 2009 by R. Gregory Christie

Carolrhoda Books
A division of Lerner Publishing Group, Inc.
241 First Avenue North
Minneapolis, MN 55401 USA

For reading levels and more information, look up this title at www.lernerbooks.com.

The images in this book are used with the permission of: © iStockphoto.com/Selahattin Bayram (jacket flaps and interior background); Western History Collections, University of Oklahoma Libraries, p. 35; Courtesy Fort Smith National Historic Site, p. 38 (top); © SuperStock, Inc./SuperStock, p. 38 (bottom).

Library of Congress Cataloging-in-Publication Data

Nelson, Vaunda Micheaux.
    Bad news for outlaws : the remarkable life of Bass Reeves, deputy U.S. marshal / by Vaunda Micheaux Nelson ; illustrations by R. Gregory Christie.
        p.   cm.
    ISBN: 978–0–8225–6764–6 (lib. bdg. : alk. paper)
    ISBN: 978–0–7613–5712–4 (EB pdf)
    1. Reeves, Bass—Juvenile literature. 2. United States marshals—Indian Territory—Biography—Juvenile literature. 3. United States marshals—Oklahoma—Biography—Juvenile literature. 4. African Americans—Oklahoma—Biography—Juvenile literature. 5. Freedmen—Oklahoma—Biography—Juvenile literature. 6. Frontier and pioneer life—Oklahoma—Juvenile literature. 7. Outlaws—Indian Territory—History—Juvenile literature. 8. Outlaws—Oklahoma—History—Juvenile literature. 9. Indian Territory—Biography—Juvenile literature. 10. Oklahoma—Biography—Juvenile literature. I. Christie, R. Gregory. II. Title.
    F697.R44N45 2008
    363.28'2092—dc22 [B]

Manufactured in the United States of America
15-48902-5568-12/16/2019

Acknowledgments for quoted material: p. 7, D. C. Gideon, *Indian Territory* (New York: Lewis Publishing Co., 1901), 117–118; p. 14, Richard D. Fronterhouse, "Bass Reeves: The Forgotten Lawman," Western History Collections (seminar paper, University of Oklahoma, Norman, 1960), 2; pp. 18, 34, Art T. Burton, *Black, Red and Deadly: Black and Indian Gunfighters on the Indian Territory, 1870–1907* (Austin, TX: Eakin Press, 1991), 156, 216, 179; p. 38, Time-Life Books, *Gunfighters of the Old West* (Alexandria, VA: Time-Life Books, 1974), 149.

FOR DREW,
who led me to Bass

FOR ART T. BURTON,
who helped me to know him

AND FOR BASS REEVES,
who was someone to ride the river with

—*V.M.N.*

FOR MARSHALL "BOY" ST. AMANT,
*a hardworking, respectable,
outspoken, and strong man*

—*R.G.C.*

SHOWDOWN

Indian Territory, 1884

Jim Webb's luck was running muddy when Bass Reeves rode into town. Webb had stayed one jump ahead of the lawman for two years. He wasn't about to be caught now. Packing both rifle and revolver, the desperado leaped out a window of Bywaters' store. He made a break for his horse, but Reeves cut him off.

Bass hollered from the saddle of his stallion, warning Webb to give up.

The outlaw bolted.

Bass shook his head. He hated bloodshed, but Webb might need killing. As a deputy U.S. marshal, it was Bass's job to bring Webb in. Alive or dead. Bass had put Webb behind bars before, but the outlaw was back on the run. That would end today.

Webb couldn't outrun a horse. And knew he'd hang for sure this time. In a last-ditch effort to escape, Webb stopped in his tracks, turned, and let loose with his rifle.

Webb's first shot grazed Bass's saddle horn. His second shot cut a button from the lawman's coat. Webb's third tore the reins right out of Bass's hands. Bass ducked his head, dove off his horse, and rolled to his feet just as a fourth bullet clipped his hat brim.

That was Jim Webb's last shot. Ever. Marshal Reeves
fired two rounds from his Winchester rifle, and the
outlaw was done for.

As he lay dying, Webb told Bass, "You are a brave,
brave man. . . . I have killed eleven men . . . and I
expected to make you the twelfth."

Webb gave Bass his revolver out of respect. Bass
buried Webb's body and turned in the outlaw's boots and
gun belt as proof he'd gotten his man.

Being a peace officer in Indian Territory was rough and dangerous. The area swarmed with horse thieves, train robbers, cattle rustlers, and gunslingers. Bandits, swindlers, and murderers thrived. Travelers sometimes disappeared, never to be heard from again. A lawman's career could be short—and end bloody.

So Bass Reeves had a big job. And it suited him right down to the ground. Everything about him was big.

Bass stood a head taller than most men of his time.
He had broad shoulders and huge hands. Bass was so strong,
he single-handedly pulled a steer out of mud up to its neck
while a bunch of slack-jawed cowpokes stood speechless.

Bass sported a large, bushy mustache and wore a wide-
brimmed black hat. He rode tall, powerful horses.

But the biggest thing about Bass Reeves was his character.
He had a dedication to duty few men could match. He didn't
have a speck of fear in him. And he was as honest as the day
is long.

Slave Days

Bass spent most of his early years as a slave in Texas.
Even as a youngster, his star shone bright. Bass was sharp-witted and good-natured. People liked his pluck. He had a special way with animals, especially horses. Bass tended livestock and fetched water for the field hands. While he worked, Bass sang. He sang about pistols and rifles and knives. He sang of bandits and killers and thieves.

His mother feared her boy might go bad. She couldn't have been more wrong. Bass took to guns like a bear to honey, but he always handled them with respect. He grew up smart and decent and had nothing but right in his heart.

His owner, Colonel George Reeves, took Bass hunting and entered him in shooting contests. He liked showing Bass off. Bass impressed his owner so much the colonel took him along when he went to fight in the Civil War.

But one night, something happened that changed everything for Bass. Folks say the two men argued during a card game, and Bass struck his owner. For a slave, this meant certain death. Bass made tracks for Indian Territory.

Freedom and Family

Late 1860s–1874

Only Native Americans were supposed to live in Indian Territory, but some Indians accepted blacks. Bass lived within the tribes, learned their languages, and perfected his marksmanship. As he roamed the frontier, Bass felt a freedom he'd never known. Still, as a runaway slave, Bass had to keep on the dodge.

Finally, the Civil War ended, and the slaves were free.
It was safe for Bass to settle down. He bought a spread in
Arkansas, just outside Indian Territory, and married a pretty
woman named Jennie. True to the song of his life, Bass had
a big family. He and Jennie and their eleven children worked
the land and raised hardy livestock.

Bass's life was good, but times were hard for folks in Indian
Territory. The vastness of this wild country offered countless
places for bad men to hide. The territory became a haven
for the West's most notorious outlaws. Settlers in Indian
Territory had had enough. Even though most were squatters
who had put down stakes illegally, they still wanted protection.

Deputy U.S. Marshal

1875–1900s

In 1875 the U.S. government sent Judge Isaac C. Parker to bring law to the territory. People called him the Hanging Judge, and the mention of his name made outlaws who'd never spent a day in church whisper a prayer. The judge hired two hundred deputy marshals to track down outlaws in an area covering 74,000 square miles, larger than what would become the entire state of Oklahoma. Bass Reeves was one of them. He became Judge Parker's most trusted man.

Bass was perfect for the job. He knew the territory and its people, downright handy tools for tracking criminals. And his skill with shooting irons was already the talk of the territory.

Bass was blazing fast on the draw and as good with his left hand as with his right. He would say he was "only fair" with a rifle. But Bass was such a crack shot, he was barred from turkey shoots at picnics and fairs. He always won. One sharpshooter said when Bass stood firm and took careful aim, "he could shoot the left hind leg off a contented fly sitting on a mule's ear at a hundred yards and never ruffle a hair."

Like most former slaves, Bass couldn't read, but this didn't stop him from doing his job. Before going after wanted men, he had the arrest warrants from Judge Parker read to him. Bass listened carefully and memorized the shapes of the letters for each name he heard. He memorized the charges against each person too. Then he'd hit the trail. Even when he got thirty warrants at one time, Bass always brought in the right outlaws.

Bass could be out man hunting for weeks. He slept on the ground under the stars and worked in bitter cold and sweltering heat. Like other deputy marshals, Bass traveled with a chuck wagon and cook, a guard, at least one posse man, and a tumbleweed wagon to transport captives.

Many lawmen of the time weren't much better than the hard cases they arrested. But Bass was as right as rain from the boot heels up. He couldn't be bribed. And he shot only as a last resort, even when Judge Parker said, "Bring them in alive—or dead!" Some outlaws, like Jim Webb, forced gunplay. Whenever Bass could, he found another way.

Bass took many a bad man by surprise through the use of disguises. One day he'd pose as a cowboy. Another he'd be a tramp, a gunslinger, or an outlaw.

Even horses played a part in his disguises. Like many U.S. marshals, Bass rode some of the finest. Most times, he forked a handsome sorrel. Bass rode proud in the saddle. There was no mistaking his silhouette. But prize horseflesh could be a dead giveaway that the rider was a lawman. Bass always kept some rough stock and rode lazy while undercover.

He planned every capture carefully.

When Bass caught wind that two outlaw brothers were holed up at their mother's cabin, he rounded up a posse and made camp some distance away. Bass knocked the heels from a pair of worn boots and shot three holes in a floppy old hat. He hid his badge, handcuffs, and pistols under trail-worn clothes, then started walking, alone, to the hideout. It was a long walk—28 miles. Bass wanted to be sure that if the brothers spotted him, they wouldn't suspect he was the law.

When the outlaws' mother answered the door, Bass said he was tuckered out and hungry. Showing the woman the bullet holes in his hat, he claimed a posse was after him. She took Bass in, fed him some vittles, and even let slip that her boys were on the lam. When the two arrived, they agreed to partner up with Bass, and after sharing some laughs, everyone went to sleep. Everyone except Bass.

At sunup, the brothers awoke in handcuffs.
They were dumbstruck, but their ma was fit to be
tied. As Bass led her sons away, she followed for
three miles, calling him every bad name she knew.

On a different warrant, Bass pretended to be a farmer. He rented some scrawny oxen and a run-down wagon. Bass drove the rig to the hideout of the men he was tracking. He ran over a stump on purpose and got a wheel caught. The outlaws came out to help. They wanted to get him away from their hideout. Just as the criminals freed up the wagon, Bass jerked his Colts. Seeing it was Deputy U.S. Marshal Bass Reeves, all four outlaws threw up their hands.

Bass brought in wagonloads of criminals, as many as seventeen prisoners at a time. Being a churchgoing man, Bass reckoned he could do more than put bad men behind bars. In the evenings after supper, he talked to the outlaws about the Bible and about doing right. Getting through to them was like trying to find hair on a frog, but Bass kept trying.

Now and then, captured outlaws tried to get the better of the marshal, but Bass was tough and unflappable.
One day, while he napped, a skunk moseyed into camp and stopped next to Bass. Captives chained to the tumbleweed wagon threw stones at the skunk, hoping it would spray its stink on the lawman. But when Bass awakened, he didn't flinch. He reached out and gently petted the skunk.

Word spread that Bass was a square shooter but a hard man. Outlaws learned that when Marshal Reeves had your warrant, you were as good as got unless you high-tailed it out of the territory. One outlaw named Hellubee Sammy did just that. With Bass on his heels, Sammy mounted a swift black charger that flat outran the marshal's sorrel. But Bass was patient. He would cross paths with Sammy on another day. And Bass would get his man.

Even the infamous "Bandit Queen" Belle Starr admired Bass.
Belle was about as far from tender as boot leather. She trifled with
the likes of Jesse James and didn't cotton to lawmen. But when she
heard Bass had her warrant, she turned herself in for the first and
only time in her long, lawless career.

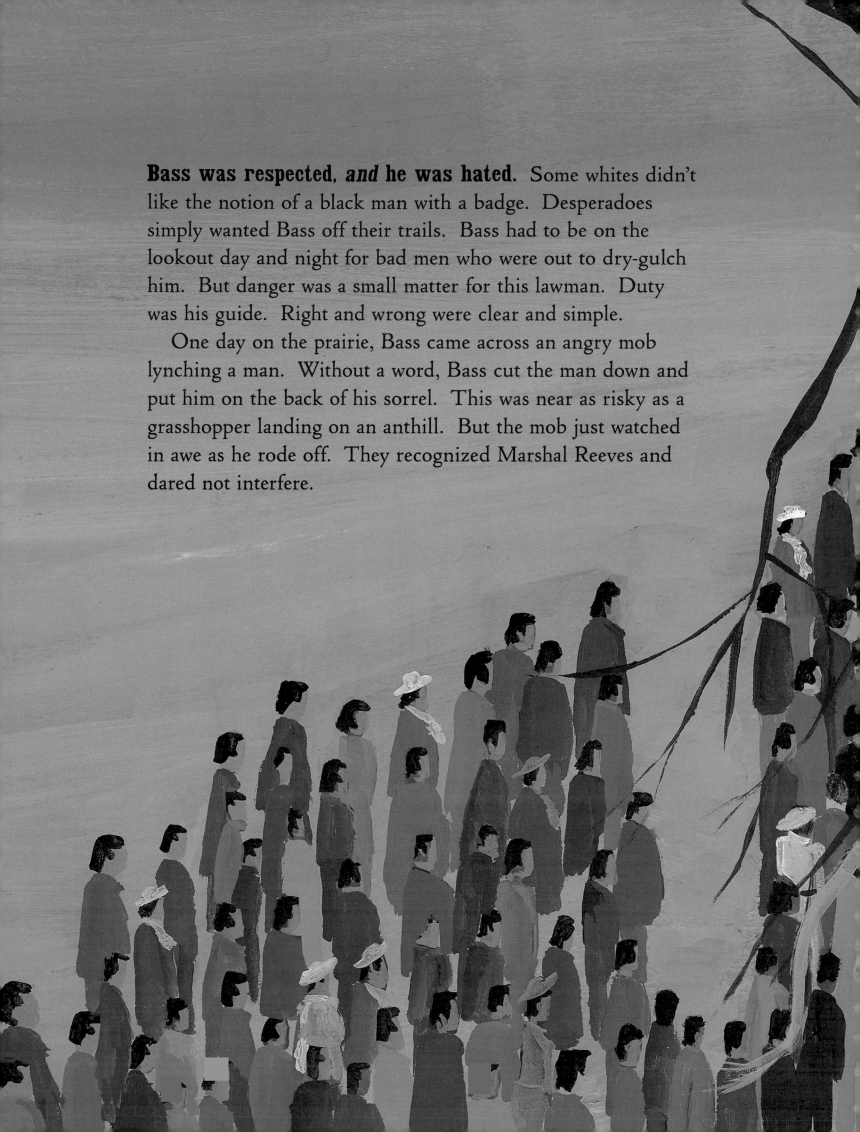

Bass was respected, *and* he was hated. Some whites didn't like the notion of a black man with a badge. Desperadoes simply wanted Bass off their trails. Bass had to be on the lookout day and night for bad men who were out to dry-gulch him. But danger was a small matter for this lawman. Duty was his guide. Right and wrong were clear and simple.

One day on the prairie, Bass came across an angry mob lynching a man. Without a word, Bass cut the man down and put him on the back of his sorrel. This was near as risky as a grasshopper landing on an anthill. But the mob just watched in awe as he rode off. They recognized Marshal Reeves and dared not interfere.

Bass's devotion to duty was legendary. His sense of justice was never more tested than by his son Benjamin. One awful day, Benjamin killed his own wife after she'd been untrue. Bass was so well liked that no one wanted to arrest his son. For two days, the warrant lay on the desk of the marshal in Muskogee. When Bass returned to the jail with prisoners, he got the sad news.

It was painful, but he did what only Bass Reeves would do. He arrested his own son and turned him over to the court. Although he was sentenced to life, Bass's son was a model prisoner and was pardoned after serving just ten years.

OKLAHOMA STATEHOOD

November 16, 1907

Bass Reeves's life as a deputy U.S. marshal ended the day Oklahoma became a state and Indian Territory ceased to exist. State and local lawmen took over the federal marshals' duties.

Bass Reeves served as deputy U.S. marshal in Indian Territory for thirty-two years, longer than any other. In fact, he was the only deputy who started with Judge Parker and stayed clear through statehood. He arrested more than three thousand men and women—blacks, whites, and Indians. Many were desperate outlaws who knew Bass "rode for Parker" and figured they had nothing to lose by fighting to the death. Bass had many close calls but was never wounded. Remarkably, he killed only fourteen men in the line of duty. Now the finest deputy U.S. marshal of his time was out of a job.

Bass bucked getting put out to pasture. He hired on with the police force in Muskogee, Oklahoma. Bass was nearly seventy years old and walking with a cane, but he still put the fear of God into lawbreakers. During his two years on the force, *not a single crime* occurred in his patrol area.

One fall day, Bass Reeves left work feeling ill.
Two months later, on January 12, 1910, he died of
a kidney ailment called Bright's disease.

Hundreds of people—blacks, whites, and
Indians—attended his burial. A fellow lawman,
Bud Ledbetter, called Bass "one of the bravest
men this country has ever known." And one white
homesteader said Bass was the "most feared deputy
U.S. marshal that was ever heard of."

Over the years, the name of Bass Reeves faded, like one of those heroes they call unsung. But his story has folks talking again. Talking about the big man who helped bring peace to a big country—Deputy U.S. Marshal Bass Reeves, a true champion of the American West.

WESTERN WORDS

chuck wagon: a wagon carrying food and supplies for cooking meals on the trail

Colts: firearms

desperado: a desperate and reckless outlaw

didn't cotton to: didn't like

dry-gulch: to lie in wait and attack someone by surprise

forked: straddled

holed up: hiding out

lynching: the crime of killing someone, often by hanging, without the approval of the law. A group of people that commits a lynching is called a lynch mob.

on the dodge (also called **on the lam**): moving from place to place to avoid capture by peace officers

peace officer: a marshal, sheriff, police officer, or other person whose job is to protect people and make sure that laws are followed

pluck: spirit or courage

posse: a group of people appointed by a sheriff or marshal to help with law enforcement, such as capturing outlaws

put down stakes: to claim a piece of land and make a home there

right as rain: honest and true

running muddy: going badly

shooting irons: firearms

sorrel: a light reddish brown horse, often with a light-colored mane and tail

spread: a ranch, or farm

square shooter: a fair and honest person

squatters: people who settle on land without a legal right

tumbleweed wagon: wagons for transporting prisoners. Tumbleweeds are dried weeds that tumble across the prairie as the wind blows. People thought that a tumbleweed wagon seemed to wander across the prairie in one direction and then another, like a tumbleweed.

vittles: food

warrant: a written document issued by a court directing an officer of the law to arrest someone or to search or seize someone's property

TIMELINE

JULY 1838
Bass Reeves is born into slavery in Arkansas but grows up in Texas.

EARLY 1860s
During the Civil War, Bass escapes to Indian Territory.

APRIL 1865
The Civil War ends. Slavery is outlawed. Bass becomes a free man.

MAY 1875
Judge Isaac C. Parker hires Bass as a deputy U.S. marshal.

JUNE 1884
Bass kills Jim Webb in the line of duty.

JANUARY 1886
Belle Starr surrenders after Bass gets her warrant.

APRIL 1889
The Indian Territory is opened to white settlement.

NOVEMBER 1896
Judge Parker dies in Fort Smith, Arkansas.

JUNE 1902
Bass arrests his son Benjamin.

NOVEMBER 1907
Oklahoma earns statehood. Bass's career as deputy U.S. marshal ends. He accepts a job on the Muskogee police force.

JANUARY 1910
Bass dies of Bright's disease.

MARCH 1992
Bass Reeves is inducted into the Hall of Great Westerners of the National Cowboy & Western Heritage Museum in Oklahoma City.

FURTHER READING AND WEBSITES

Fort Smith National Historic Site
http://www.nps.gov/fosm/index.htm
Located in Fort Smith, Arkansas, near the Oklahoma border, this park maintains the courthouse and other buildings from the time of Judge Parker. Starting in 2011, the park will host the U.S. Marshals Museum.

Kent, Deborah. *The Trail of Tears*. Danbury, CT: Children's Press, 2007. This book describes the forced march of Native Americans into Indian Territory.

Markel, Rita J. *Your Travel Guide to America's Old West*. Minneapolis: Twenty-First Century Books, 2004. This book gives readers an idea of what to eat, what to wear, and what life was like in the American West.

Oklahoma Historical Society
http://www.okhistory.org/kids/index.htm
The kids section of this website has information, games, and photos about Oklahoma's history.

Paulsen, Gary. *The Legend of Bass Reeves*. New York: Laurel-Leaf, 2008. This book contains an imagined tale of Bass Reeves's boyhood and a fictionalized account of his later life.

Underwood, Deborah. *Nat Love*. Minneapolis: Lerner Publications Company, 2008. This story of Nat Love, an African American cowboy, is based largely on his autobiography.

U.S. Marshal Service
http://www.usmarshals.gov/usmsforkids/index.html
This site gives an overview of the long history of U.S. marshals.

MORE ABOUT JUDGE ISAAC C. PARKER

During his twenty-one years at the federal court at Fort Smith, Judge Isaac C. Parker tried 13,490 cases and sent 79 lawbreakers to the gallows to be hanged. Though feared by many, Judge Parker was a just man who opposed the death penalty. But he believed in strict obedience to the law—and the law said that some crimes had to be punished with death. Judge Parker told prisoners, "I do not desire to hang you men. It is the law." While Indians generally resented white people, they saw the judge as their friend and protector. In 1896 Congress closed Judge Parker's court at Fort Smith. Six weeks later, he died of a heart attack at the age of fifty-eight.

MORE ABOUT INDIAN TERRITORY

Indian Territory became home to Native Americans who, in the 1830s, were forcibly moved there by the U.S. government. The Cherokee, Chickasaw, Choctaw, Creek, and Seminole came to be known as the Five Civilized Tribes because they adopted white ways. For some this included schools, housing, clothing, and even keeping black slaves.

Not all blacks in Indian Territory were slaves. And, in general, the Indians treated their slaves more kindly than whites did, sometimes like family members. Indians and blacks married and had children. Still, the slaves were not free.

After the Civil War, some Indians gave land to their former slaves. Many of these new landowners, along with other blacks who had migrated there, formed their own communities. By 1870 there were five black towns in Indian Territory with more to come. Although whites were not supposed to settle there, many moved into the territory illegally.

Before Judge Parker arrived, tribal police and a few deputy U.S. marshals enforced the law. But Indian police had no power to deal with lawbreakers who were not Indian. And there weren't nearly enough marshals to control the huge area. The scarcity of peace officers attracted outlaws, gamblers, whiskey peddlers, swindlers, and squatters. Because government officials secretly wanted whites to settle Indian Territory, they didn't make the squatters leave. Instead, they sent Judge Parker and his deputy U.S. marshals to make the area safe.

ABOUT THE RESEARCH

While information about Bass Reeves is considerable, some details of his life were difficult to verify. His date of birth and the story surrounding his escape from slavery are examples. In these cases, I used the most reliable material that current scholarship has uncovered. The facts of Bass's life, including all dialogue, are supported by documented sources.

Selected Bibliography

BOOKS

Brady, Paul L. *The Black Badge: Deputy United States Marshal Bass Reeves from Slave to Heroic Lawman.* Los Angeles: Milligan Books, 2005.

Burton, Art T. *Black, Red and Deadly: Black and Indian Gunfighters on the Indian Territory, 1870–1907.* Austin, TX: Eakin Press, 1991.

————. *Black Gun, Silver Star: The Life and Legend of Frontier Marshal Bass Reeves.* Lincoln: University of Nebraska Press, 2006.

Gideon, D. C. *Indian Territory.* New York: Lewis Publishing Co., 1901.

Katz, William Loren. *Black People Who Made the Old West.* New York: Thomas Y. Crowell Company, 1977.

Shirley, Glenn. *Law West of Fort Smith: A History of Frontier Justice in the Indian Territory, 1834–1896.* New York: Henry Holt and Company, 1957.

Teall, Kaye, ed. *Black History in Oklahoma: A Resource Book.* Oklahoma City: Oklahoma City Public Schools, 1971.

Trachtman, Paul. *Gunfighters of the Old West.* With the editors of Time-Life Books. Alexandria, VA: Time-Life Books, 1974.

West, C. W. "Dub." *Outlaws and Peace Officers of Indian Territory.* Muskogee, OK: Muskogee Publishing Co., 1987.

ARTICLES

Littlefield, Daniel F., Jr., and Lonnie E. Underhill. "Negro Marshals in the Indian Territory." *The Journal of Negro History,* April 1971, 77–87.

Mooney, Charles W. "Bass Reeves, Black Deputy U.S. Marshal." *Real West,* July 1976, 48–51.

Williams, Nudie E. "Bass Reeves: Lawman in the Western Ozarks." *Negro History Bulletin,* April–June 1979, 37–39.

————. "Black Men Who Wore the Star." *Chronicles of Oklahoma,* Spring 1981, 83–90.

MANUSCRIPTS

Fronterhouse, Richard D. "Bass Reeves: The Forgotten Lawman." Seminar paper, Western History Collections, University of Oklahoma Library, Norman, 1960.

Williams, Nudie E. "A History of the American Southwest: Black United States Deputy Marshals in the Indian Territory, 1875–1907." Master of arts thesis, Oklahoma State University Library, Stillwater, 1973.

INTERVIEWS

Burton, Art T. (professor of history, South Suburban College, South Holland, IL). Interviewed by the author at his home in Phoenix, IL, June 24, 2005.

AUTHOR'S NOTE
Finding Bass

I was first introduced to the Old West by the television and movie westerns of my childhood. My siblings and I watched them all—*The Lone Ranger, Hopalong Cassidy, Roy Rogers, Gunsmoke, The Rifleman, Bonanza*—anything that involved good guys, bad guys, horses, and shootouts.

We spent hours playing cowboys, eating beans from a can around a make-believe campfire, and straddling whatever we could imagine was a horse. Looking back, I remember an occasional black character in these shows, but never in the roles *we* aspired to play. I came to believe there were few blacks in the West and none who did anything I would have called important.

When I grew older, I learned about the bravery of buffalo soldiers and about black cowboys like Bill Pickett and Nat Love. Then one day in 2003 my husband, an admirer of the Old West, introduced me to Bass Reeves, a black deputy U.S. marshal. I immediately wanted to know more, and my search began.

I found information about Bass in books and articles. But there was nothing factual for children except two pages in a book called *Rough and Ready Outlaws and Lawmen* by A. S. Gintzler. Thanks to historian Art T. Burton and others who are keeping Bass's story alive, I am able to help pass it on.

Many of the western heroes we idolized as children were fictional characters, dramatized by Hollywood. But Bass Reeves was real. How different my childhood view of myself might have been if, when choosing who got the best parts, we'd fought over who got to play Bass Reeves.

Bass's story is so incredible it comes close to sounding like a tall tale. But it isn't. It's true. And I've done my best to tell it true.

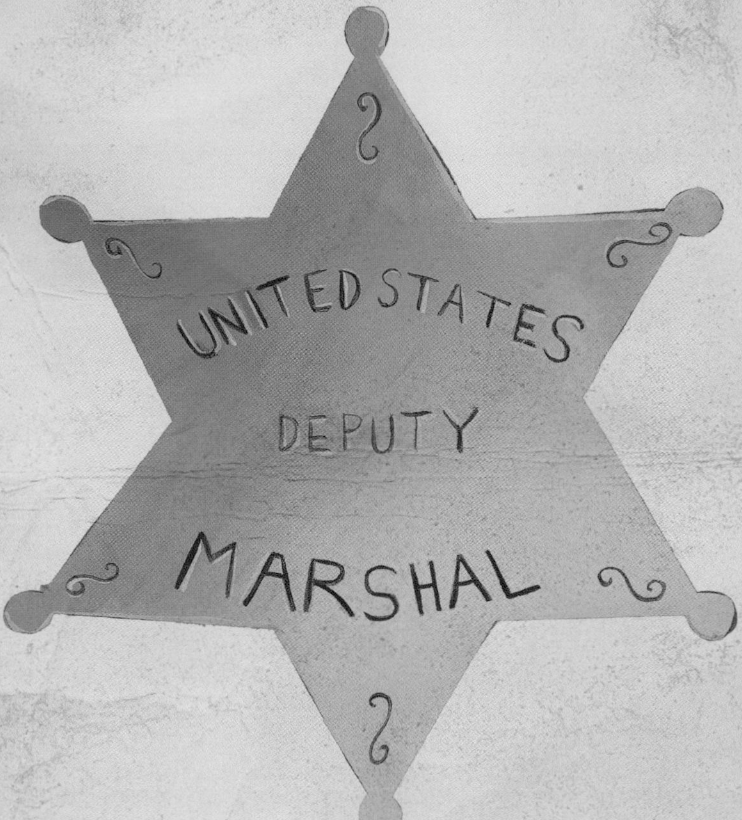
UNITED STATES
DEPUTY
MARSHAL